The Fear of Love

David Filer

Plain View Press
http://plainviewpress.net

3800 N. Lamar, Suite 730-260
Austin, TX 78756

Copyright © 2012 David Filer. All rights reserved under International and Pan-American Copyright Conventions. No part of this book may be reproduced or distributed in any form or by any means, or stored in a data base or retrieval system, without written permission from the author. All rights, including electronic, are reserved by the author and publisher.

ISBN: 978-1-935514-81-7
Library of Congress Control Number: 2012933419

Cover art photos by David Filer
Cover design by Pam Knight

To my wife, Marlene Anderson

Acknowledgments

Snow Down River
"Spring-Osprey" in *The Oregonian* (date unknown) and *The Landscape There*, Stone City Press, 2009. "Blue Heron Through Binoculars" in *Slant* (2003) and *Legal Studies Forum* (2003). "Night Verse" in *The Café Review* (2001) and *Night Verse*, Finishing Line Press (2005). "Time" in *The Landscape There*, Stone City Press (2009). "Phenomena" in *The Grove Review* (2004) and *Night Verse*, Finishing Line Press (2005). "Old Apples" in *Clackamas Literary Review* (2002) and *Night Verse*, Finishing Line Press (2005). "Snow Down River" in *The Oregonian* (2002), *Legal Studies Forum* (2003) and *Night Verse*, Finishing Line Press (2005). "One Crow Staying Back" in *Talking River Review* (2001) and *The Landscape There*, Stone City Press (2009). "Crow Blackbirds" in *White Pelican Review* (2007). "Warning" in *Gumball Poetry* (2003) and *The Landscape There*, Stone City Press (2009). "Winter Burning" in *Spring Hill Review* (2003) and *The Landscape There*, Stone City Press (2009). "October 26, 2002" in *Red River Review* (2003). "Full Moon, Mid-July" in *The Café Review* (2001). "In Darkness It Flashes" in *Night Verse*, Finishing Line Press (2005). "Mood Indigo: Holding Steady" in *The Café Review* (2002).

The Fear of Love
"Still Life" in *Gumball Poetry* (2003). "Portrait" in *Weather Patterns*, Dancing Moon Press (2011). "Evening" in *Zyzzyva* (2003), *The Landscape There*, Stone City Press (2009) and *Housekeeping*, Finishing Line Press (2012). "Triangulation" in *Fireweed* (2000). "Impatience" in *Brevities* (2007). "Sonnets To My Father" in *PoetSpeak* (2004) and *Into the Teeth of the Wind* (2004), *The Landscape There*, Stone City Press (2009) and *Housekeeping*, Finishing Line Press (2012). "Beverly" in *Poetry Depth Quarterly* (2007). "August: A Vow" in *The Landscape There* (2009). "Aubade" in *The Oregonian* (ca. 2000) and *Night Verse*, Finishing Line Press (2005). "Storm Front" in *The Oregonian* (ca. 2000) and *Night Verse*, Finishing Line Press (2005).

Travel Notes
"View" in *Exit 13* (#18 Spring 2012). "While Reading James' *The Golden Bowl* at the Bus Stop" in *Weather Patterns*, Dancing Moon Press (2011). "Calle Garcia Vigil" in *Cider Press Review* (2005) and *Night Verse*, Finishing Line Press (2005). "Bugby Hole" in *Weather Patterns*, Dancing Moon Press (2011). "Cathlamet Pastoral" in *James River Poetry Review* (2003). "The Jazz at Jimmy Mak's" in *Cider Press Review* (2005) and *Night Verse*,

Finishing Line Press (2005). "Postcard from Shaniko" in *The Landscape There*, Stone City Press (2009). "Japanese Garden" in *Brevities* (2007) and *Weather Patterns*, Dancing Moon Press (2011). "Photographs" in *Tiger's Eye* (2007). "Self-Guided" in *Weather Patterns*, Dancing Moon Press (2011). "Itinerary" in *Tiger's Eye* (2007). "Three Wedding Quatrains" in *Weather Patterns*, Dancing Moon Press (2011). "Aubade" in *The Café Review* (2008). "Portland Time" in *Gumball Poetry* (2003). "Shining Back" in *The Sow's Ear* (2003), *Night Verse*, Finishing Line Press (2005) and *Housekeeping*, Finishing Line Press (2012). "Diminishing" (as "Sonnets Diminishing") in *Untitled Country Review* (2011) and *Housekeeping*, Finishing Line Press (2012). "Since You Asked" in *The Oregonian* (2008) and *Weather Patterns*, Dancing Moon Press (2011).

Postscripts
"Late Elegy" in *Wild Goose Poetry Review* (2007), *The Landscape There*, Stone City Press (2009) and *Housekeeping*, Finishing Line Press (2012).

Contents

Snow Down River   9

    Spring – Osprey   11
    Blue Heron Through Binoculars   12
    Night Verse   13
    Time   15
    Phenomena   16
    Old Apples   18
    Snow Down River   20
    One Crow Staying Back   22
    Crow Blackbirds   24
    Warning   25
    Winter Burning   26
    Setting   27
    October 26, 2002   28
    Full Moon, Mid-July   29
    In Darkness It Flashes   31
    Mood Indigo: Holding Steady   33

The Fear of Love   35

    Still Life   37
    Letter Listing Reasons   38
    Portrait   39
    Funambulist   40
    Evening   41
    Triangulation   42
    The Fear of Love   43
    Aftershock   46
    Impatience   47
    Sonnets to My Father   48
    Beverly   49
    When It Is Late and Quiet   50
    August: A Vow   51
    Sketch: Dandelions   54
    Event of Note: March 27, 2004   55

Aubade	59
Storm Front	60

Travel Notes   61

View	63
While Reading James' *The Golden Bowl* at the Bus Stop	65
Calle Garcia Vigil	66
Bugby Hole	68
Poem Addressed to Passengers on the Downtown Bus	69
Return Trip	71
Cathlamet Pastoral	72
The Jazz at Jimmy Mak's	75
Travel Notes	78
Postcard from Shaniko	80
Japanese Garden, Portland Oregon	82
Photographs	83
Self-Guided	84
It Happened	85
Weather Notes	87
Itinerary	89
Atcheson, Topeka and Santa Fe	93
Three Wedding Quatrains	95
The Mortals of Keşan	96
Aubade	99
Portland Time	100
Shining Back	101
Diminishing	102
Since You Asked	103

Postscripts   105

Late Elegy	107
Taken	108
Epitaph in Advance	109

Poem Notes	111
About the Author	113

Snow Down River

Spring–Osprey

The way April is
in this landscape.

Mid-afternoon sun
cuts through the chaos
of clouds, exploding
the light-green of new
cottonwoods between dark
slough water and the fir-banked
palisades. Just in that
moment of thought,

a quick west wind
streaks across the slough,
and the osprey
backs against it,
takes a long
look into the shallow
water below.

Spring's keen hunger
holding in
the edgy wind.

David Filer

Blue Heron Through Binoculars

The slough sparkles silver and black
in the evening sun, as if shards
of light floated in the river at dusk.

A heron strides slowly, ruffled
breast and belly at the water-line,
the tide ebbing slowly as his pace.

Now the stillness, the wait, head
and dagger-beak cocked taut and ready.
Silence is what I see in that focused

place, though where I am, the breeze
rattles through old cottonwood leaves.
The tall grass heads hiss. Scrub jays

argue back and forth between the dog-
wood and the old apple where the feeder
is hung. Copeland's Appalachian Spring

seeps out through the back deck doors.
Odd how its keening lines weave skeins
of dread through the hopeful melodies:

sound always defining a fading past.
Does the heron hear in this moment?
or does hunger concentrate his world

into a pure circle of sight, a sharp,
soundless present, so that the wind's
random voices have become mute?

Through the glass, the heron waits,
poised, its silence awesome: something
needed out there, gleaming, coming closer.

Night Verse

> *Each verse returning like the plough turned round.*
>   Seamus Heaney, "Glanmore Sonnet No. 2"

To Marlene

Last night,
while you were sleeping,
your back pressed
into my chest, I
listened to that tractor
disking the long pasture
across the road.
And under the diesel's
coarse drone, I heard
the small song

of the meadow-vole
moving carefully through
the dry grass.
The long-fingered song
of the raccoon,
probing at low tide
for a meal of fresh-
water clams.
And the edgy song
of the white-tailed

deer, out from dogwood
cover to eat
the apples we
collected and spread
under the willow.
And I heard
the cottonwoods' dry
leaves, and the mist
rising from the slough
near dawn.

David Filer

In that sweet
harmony, tuned
by your sleep,
I lay there,
and listened to each
verse the tractor
made, and to the text
of that August night
cut, turned, and left
shining under the clear
new moon.

Time

> *Time watches from the shadow...*
>   W.H. Auden, "As I walked out one evening"

Deer are in the back yard again.
Tense. White tails twitching. They head
For the old apple tree. But it's

December, a full month since
The last ones fell. Those apples
Were like dreams, cold sweet fruit

Under troubled skin. I'd check
Too, come out into the open.
The past is easily forgotten.

Hearts hunger, back in their gnarled
Undergrowth, while the garden
Hardens in the clear, dry air.

Above, the owl knows, pale light
Moving through bare cottonwoods.
Geese startle into noisy flight

Out in the slough, circle, then
Settle back in silence. The blind vole
Turns in her damp burrow. Time

Edges upward always, touching
Every taproot, from the molten pulse
Deep within the wintered world.

David Filer

Phenomena

For Bob Reynolds

Suddenly this rain,
sweeping across the island
sometimes hissing
on the edge of hail.
Here I am, inside,
lawn still not mowed,
next winter's firewood
half split and stacked,
the rest—grains and gnarls
intact—scattered around
the splitting block.
Nothing to do but stay
dry and wait.

Next door, there is no
waiting. Time slips away
like a skim of clouds.
My old neighbor gets up
to talk and never speaks
of the pain it causes,
speaks of memory instead.
You should keep a daybook,
he says. Write down what's
here so you don't have
the trouble I have.

The trouble I have
is rain from the west.
But it will pass through,
and evening, longer now
in late April, will clear
along the Oregon hills.
I will sit on the porch.
I will do as he said,
I will write things down:

The Fear of Love

In the fragile light,
a hen pheasant will step
out from the dry dogwood
bramble, become visible
against the deep spring
grass, then vanish
with its next step.

David Filer

Old Apples

> *...this great curved surface of dread...*
> John Updike

Deer have eaten
the lowest. Others
marred by weather

and lack of care. Late
November, dark
red and barely

hanging from cold-
stripped branches,
a few can be picked,

tart but worth eating,
after the damage
has been pared away.

◯

Old apples.
They hang on dry stems,
in angled winter light.

Air thins between
them and the wet grass.
The earth waits.

Sequined in brown
leaves, it curves up
from its horrid center,

imperceptible,
and without a sound.
Whole days

pass and nothing
changes. Then, as if
they have become

the text of an old
painting, there
is nothing to change.

◯

A new history begins.
I remember it both
ways, now. The gnarled

shapes, the damage,
the tart white pulp just
beneath taut skin.

Cold, and the way
time holds. Leaves
littering a swollen earth.

I remember it
like a dream, then, a dream
of you, the last

words you said, hanging
there, in that still
air at year's end.

David Filer

Snow Down River

> *How hard to be as human as snow…*
> Charles Wright, "Disjecta Membra"

I haven't seen it snow
this far down river in years.

I know the occasional weather
that makes it: jet stream
bends to the north, the last
rain moves on east, and the valley
fills with frigid air.

Days of this, under misleading
sun, and then more rain,
freezing as it falls. And so

this shawl of snow, slowing
like a message as it falls,
spreading across the boggy,
river-rimmed fields,
shading them first to gray,
then white, and deeper white.

It isn't why it snows,
it's why it snows now,
snow some kind of sign

for this year's end, weather
that unifies, defining gardens
and grazing fields as one,

bare alder, ash and willow,
lawns and dry river grass
as one, highway and road
bending back to the barn
as one, until the island

floats in silence and thought,
like hope for a quiet year, river
flowing by and on down to the sea.

        Christmas, 2001

David Filer

One Crow Staying Back

For Bob Reynolds

Old neighbor,
you told me about the black
gathering,

in your yard
at mid-week, when the late
summer day

was quiet
and the lawn, sloping down
to the water,

was open
for the stark business
of crows.

◯

There were a number
of them, down from the cottonwoods—
the kind of crows,

I take it,
that loom and cackle in the snarled
branches

of your dreams,
crows ready to take some of the blame.
And you noticed

that sometimes,
just when there are plenty of them
gathered,

The Fear of Love

and you step out
to bitch back, they leave, with a great
argument of wings.

◯

All except one,
especially ornery or outcast, hard to tell,
but it stays,

shoulders hunched,
feathers out-of-align, lifting one claw, then the other
from the short grass.

And there he is,
black silhouette against faded summer green,
the one crow

staying back,
intent yellow eyes, and ragging voice you will know
when it comes time.

David Filer

Crow Blackbirds

> *The Crow Blackbird is…a poor bird to have about the house if other more attractive species are desired.*
> P.A. Taverner, *Birds of Western Canada*

They are here again this evening. They are always here, but it is evenings they gather as they are, in that row of dark green pines across the road, or in the cottonwoods at the corner of the property. The crows. The crow blackbirds. They have been here and they have been everywhere, all day.

They have been across the split river—its swirls and flotsam carried high with the tide and spring flood—to the Washington side, where the palisades give way to the west, Cathlamet, then down to the slow Elochoman, delta still full of winter ducks.

They have stood beside the road, ebony heads shining, strutting out between pickups, the morning milk truck, the contract mail carrier weaving back and forth, mailbox to mailbox. They have gathered some sustenance from the road's small casualties. They have sought out the unprotected smaller lives from nests and dodged the red-wings' frantic feints and thrusts.

But when evening tilts the light low across the long green pastures—sheep now settled far back under the maples, a few white-tailed deer grazing in their place—when the clouds dissolve into the deckled sky, and when the wind slows and steam from the Wauna mill glows against the dark Oregon hills:

Then they gather as they are in the dark green pines or nearby cottonwoods. Crows. Crow blackbirds. Like a raucous syndicate of nightmares, waiting to enter into dreams.

The Fear of Love

Warning

Fog drifts along the palisades, pouring through dark firs
at the crest. The light is gravestone on the slough. Herons

are out of sorts, standing on pilings instead of mud,
keeping their long legs dry. The wind is contrary, headed

the opposite way of the river. If you put your ear down
to the rising water, you will hear what is coming to my heart.

It makes the same sound as granite, scraping down
from the mountains in the cold depths of the current;

sometimes, like the muffled tumbling of a deep snag,
years working its way downstream, where it will surprise

fishermen who have never had trouble casting there. If you
have never heard it before, still, you will know why I have been

forgetful of ordinary courtesies, and why I get up before
dawn and check how many apples have fallen. Then you,

too, will know to be wary; and, like the herons, you
will find somewhere to stand above the foreseeable tide.

David Filer

Winter Burning

There is no breeze. Persistent
fog seals the fine edge
between earth and heaven. A ship
plies the channel, headed
out to sea, its horn
marking the passage, mile by mile.

Now when it blows,
it's west, below the island,
and moving out
of range. Otherwise,
no sound, except the snap
and flutter of the fire

I've been tending
all afternoon—now in darkness,
a mound of amber coals—
and the light, dry
rattle of the few maple leaves
left in early December,

their signal faint
in the growing cold,
and above, where the fire's
sparks rise and dim,
the call of tundra swans
navigating home.

Setting

To see what it is,
nothing more than stillness,
like this water held
at high tide, the creak
and chuckle of blackbirds
in an old willow,
a few loosestrife blooming
at the ends of their stalks.

It had a name once,
but it has flown off
like the quarter-moon
that hovers at dusk
just above the ridge
in the west:

As if a face
turned just enough to see
both ways.

It may become dark
and there may be ash,
or a song taken up
a few notes at a time.

Too early.
Too early to tell.

David Filer
October 26, 2002

Afternoon the day before we turn time
back. Sun—low west of the house behind me—
paints a palette of fall color across
the lawn, water, dry river grass and reeds.
Cottonwoods half-turned, half-green. Farther
off, maples scattered among the dark firs
on the slope up to the palisades. All
shades of amber anxious to let go, color
seeping to the very air, as if lightened
by fall into a memory of itself.
It made me think of you, fading away
as time moves on, but lingering still.
A warm third season here, but turning cool.

The Fear of Love

Full Moon, Mid-July

Two nights
of barking dogs,
then the tide peaks,
taking seriously

that old inclination.
Buoy-chains
straighten and grow
taut; snags stir like old

men in sleep, wander,
then settle
their crooked joints
into softer mud.

☽

How the night changes;
how the stars open,
like songs,
into the keen distance.

The breeze
is fatherless, motherless,
electric, whispering
like white owls in the dark

cottonwoods. Mist rises
like a dream
in the differential
between water and air.

☽

It is too late to go
back. All night
the mountains
wear away

David Filer

and are brought down
in the deep
channels. Dawn cuts
across our sleep.

We forget promises. Like
pirates, we
withdraw seaward,
eddies of night, running
out through valleys of mud.

◓

What we remember is what
we take away,
steeped in damp clothes,
like a lesser tide, moving again.

Later, we have stories,
words gathered
above the tidal zone,
stacked and fired in the early

morning cold. A rustling, a faint
note: wren's song,
day moving down
the palisades.

In Darkness It Flashes

*To will it is enough to take
Them there.*
        Donald Justice, "Women in Love"

To Marlene

She wanted angels
in her life, with prayers
like the soft movement
of birds, susurrus
of quick, accurate
wings, come back from some
distant place, precisely
when needed, lacing
the still evening air.

They came, and also small
green and yellow frogs,
chanting in the dusk
from under dogwoods,
from the muddy swale
across the dike road,
starting and stopping
in unison, and on
into the July night.

Neither could she doubt
that they were angels
she was blessed with:
these ephemera,
these seasonal hymns
in ditch and air around
her, though walking there,
she could see mere purple
wings, yellow throats, hear

David Filer

their ordinary song.
See how she brings
the collar of her coat
up around her neck,
as light fades and mist
thickens in the cooling
air, and how even
in darkness it flashes
like a cape of stars.

Mood Indigo: Holding Steady

Sometimes, I could leave The Dock early
On a Saturday night, and start across
The Cathlamet Bridge, looking straight south,
Into a sky that was the last color
Of blue before dark. Some would have said the light
Was gone and it was night, but it was not,
Because the sky was blue, that last color
Of blue before dark. It was mid-summer,
And perhaps it would have been impossible
Then to be sure night would ever come, if one
Had to say that there was no light at all.
And that was what it looked like, looking south:
As if the sky would always be, perhaps,
That last color of blue before dark.

The Fear of Love

Still Life

> *Every life is many days…*
> James Joyce, *Ulysses*

Through the limits of the sun
the stream runs down by itself
and we do not expect more.

If we are all
suddenly someone
else, what difference?
By chance you would
climb
past the timberline,
sit through a morning
on old granite.

Even as you stand dressed
in a smock before your students
discussing brush strokes,
here, the wheat fields are broken,
sheaves stacked in lines of crosses.
A moth
flies at the soft light
behind my door,
falls,
scuds off into
darkness.

        Çorlu Turkey, 1968

David Filer

Letter Listing Reasons

To Marlene

There are reasons I love
the fence-climbing rose,
the night-blooming jasmine

you planted beside the front
porch, its scent
emerging in the spring air.

I know I should love
the dark green speedwell,
tiny white watercress,

flat mudwort exposed
on sand bars, in summer
low tides, wapato, yellow

water-flag that scatters hard
mahogany seeds in late
fall, small flowered forget-

me-nots transplanted by the pier,
purple loosestrife, heavy-
headed nodding beggarticks,

bog trefoil, pennyroyal, toad-
rush, cow parsnip, the brief
pink nookta rose of early

May. But enough, these too
are reasons I love your
domestic rose, your night-

blooming jasmine settled
by the porch, their scents
gracing the still evening air.

Portrait

She sits alone, eyes
motionless, yet with a cat's
stare, circling into the tended
garden her silence creates.

Iris sway at the edge
of sight. Music plays faintly
there and defines her grace.

Beyond the neat rows
and carefully pruned stems
are shadows where she
has been desired—dark like
her latent screams, vanishing
before she allows herself
to be embraced.

David Filer

Funambulist

> *...if I walk it with artistry, with poetry...*
> Philippe Petit

Here is a rope of words, thin as a new idea, straight as a plowed field, spun cable cold to your calloused foot, a mere thread, as Stafford said, a gossamer, a road a runway off into the unknown. Step off there, foot before foot, slowly until the rope's rhythm becomes yours, the sway and torque learned by the muscle, memorized in the inner ear. Make your pace graceful, considerate, sure, one with the unthinkable space above, the more dangerous space below, all compressed to the moment of your next footfall.

Step off on these words—loosestrife, yellow-flag, cottonwoods turning pale green, a late spring hailstorm—and you step off on an island, where downstream, the heart waits, watching the river split, bringing something down in its eddied drift.

Step off on these words, and feel the subtle rush of water past your ear, center lane, Redmond Municipal Pool, half-way through a 3000 meter swim, when you realize you will not stay married, clear current carrying away the tears.

Step off on these words, step carefully where a few old apples hang on a cold, November day, sun low in the sky, and the rope leads to where you happen to be, trembling, coming to terms with time.

Here is your rope of words. Walk out over the chasm, trust in your feet and slender frame, balance with your bending pole of thought. You know it is the walking that counts, one foot and then one foot and yet one foot, and when you arrive at that small place at the other end, it will just be a place to step off from again, on another rope of words.

Evening

> *Every old thing is with me…*
>   Reginald Gibbons, "The Voice Of Someone Else"

Every old thing is with me, when I let
The evening in, with all its histories.
Venus just now an hour from her set,
Bright above hills and fog. Wind skims the trees,
Hissing as if static, and then signals
Coming from somewhere, crossing the space
Imagination frames, pulses sweet and full,
Like memories I know I should not waste.
Where are you now, what have you learned,
That you're here in this unfamiliar place?
I'm looking west, to a sky growing dark
And cold, all but the planet's lamp-like trace.
Somehow your faded voice has touched me here.
How distant love can be and still be near.

David Filer

Triangulation

> *To Curran and Neal*
> September 1995

I have seen the Susquehanna
and imagine it now in late summer, water
low and sluggish, maples green, fields

already disked for Fall. Navigation
is the art of placement, resolving doubt. So
when my father called and asked had

I heard from you, I could explain:
you had not been there long and would report
in once your routines were sure.

I thought of him in Ojai, looking
westward past the dark oak hills, silhouetted
in the late evening light. Out

there, beyond sight, is the sea,
and as the air cools, fog burgeons
into the valley, spreading

as the sun recedes. He thinks
about you now, and sees something, wishes
he had more time to watch.

In Portland, where it has been
dry but cool, forecasts of winter rain
still weeks away,

I sight east and south, down two legs
of that triangle that fixes the location of my heart,
thankful while some clear weather holds.

The Fear of Love

> *and being what we are we chose love*
> *and having found it we lost it over and over*
> Philip Levine, "Salt"

Fall storm cottonwoods yellow
leaves wild in the southwest wind
grasses dogwood bent sprung back
bent again under the next
gust old tumult of weather
lost days words lost faces and that
one partially in the darkened
theater coming through the crowd
that one could be real or
just the old persistent dream.

☾

When I lie here alone wind rising
into higher chords through bare trees

the tremor is like words the hum
of words heard through two doors

down a long hall remembered now
the sound the river makes wearing

mountains down into sand thought listened
to carefully until it is no longer heard.

☾

I remember the desert
air at night the dark thin somehow
stars always in winter how long
and cold the block was walking
all the way around before
trying the front door I wake
in a heavier night now years

David Filer

later a Pacific storm humming
through the bare trees rain eddying
against the east window you
are asleep beside me turn speak
some words that only half emerge
I have been up twice unable
to leave the dream a harbor
bridge off in the distant mist
nowhere near here nowhere
near this rushing silence.

☾

Mist and rain all day
last hours of October
cold Chopin falling

through the yellow leaves
like something lost returning
singing on the street.

☾

At the corner some-
one has left an old mattress
leaning against the fire

hydrant how long I
don't know what war love has waged
on its horrid springs.

☾

There are hand-made signs
on the power poles lost last
night a fragile truth

this morning starlings
click and fidget through the canes
of old blackberries.

○

White crocus again
startling in the dark winter
mud opening like

a reflection like
a girl's face seen briefly through
an upstairs window.

○

Finally I have moved
the stones who thought spreading stones
would be easier

than rain songs lost love
than memory of that face
smooth gray river stones.

○

Sleep came late
after the winds died

morning early
January

spread cold and copper
over the palisades

tide rising and eight dove
silhouetted in the ash

making it easy to remain
making it easy.

David Filer

Aftershock

The space once
  filled with comfort
remains
  when comfort
dies.

A room emptied
  with outlines of rug
and furniture
  still on the hard
wood floors.

The neural
  memory of limbs
severed
  a hand no longer

there aching
  in the cold.
Too sudden always
  death finds us

unprepared to forget
  the taste of
milk on
  a warm
breast.

Impatience

One can touch it, skin
and hair: taste the salt,
brittle, dry iris
blossoms, mid-day heat.

But struggle to find
ordinary words
for feelings which well
up like tears in Spring.

It leaves: a rustle,
a recollection;
not quite cedar bark,
wind-swept ocean spume.

David Filer

Sonnets to My Father

He's eighty-four, and still he's going strong.
That's what I say, but he complains of loss
Of strength. So he pushes out his daily walk
A block, then two, and soon he's gone so long
He cannot remember where he's been. Then
It's yard work, laundry, and now, he's in the car
And off for groceries. He says: It's not far.
Never at night. He says: Don't worry. I spend
My time carefully. He says: I won't be wired
Again to that pulsing screen, that urine bag.
That's your nightmare, too. Forget it. That sag
In the last ridge, seaward. See it? That's where
I'll be when that sharp flutter comes again.
He says: Let's walk. Bring your jacket. I smell rain.

And we still walk, though no longer together,
Not to that last ridge where he stands and shows
Me the sea. He's more like a shadow now,
Thrown from behind, each year getting longer.
And is it his—gaunt, stooping, with a pot
Belly—or is it mine? Harder to tell
Each year. Harder to break the growing spell
I thought I'd broken years ago. Not
That I'm becoming him. I know better.
Though sometimes it's him I see while shaving,
And I hear his rasp in my own talking.
Time's made us distant and now we're closer.
He's with me even when he's not along.
He's passed on now, but still he's going strong.

Beverly

Sometimes, when people
go who we do not

want to lose, they are
replaced. Not a true

reincarnation,
but something that keeps

their awe present. So,
the sudden wingbeat

and taut wire-like pluck
of the hummingbird,

body iridescent
in the slanting sun,

brought her back to us.
We could not but look.

But then, as if we
shouldn't have, or looked

too long, she vanished.
It was time enough:

for that quick song,
we were flowers again,

and remembered
our blossoming hearts.

David Filer

When It Is Late and Quiet

To Marlene

I hear you up there above,
first to bathroom, then across
the hall to bed, old wooden
floors giving away your path.

Outside, a steady winter
rainstorm pelts roof and windows.
The moon glows above dense clouds.
Beyond that, planets circle

a sun we see little of
this time of year. Farther still,
galaxies spin out to the vast
unknowable edge of time.

When it is late and quiet,
layers emerge: a cold maze
winding into the heavens,
where I go, alone in thought.

The way back is to your side,
gravity pulling me down
toward your center, where you lie
turning inside a dream.

You hold my orbit, as you sleep,
and mutter, in the darkness,
words that become poetry
when I wander through the night.

August: A Vow

To Curran and Young
August 19, 2006

1

The weather has turned.
Sun slipped down
to the south without

warning. Wind rattles
dry fescue, red-tails
stalk the brown pastures.

Cottonwood leaves drop.
Yellow iris pods
split, their mahogany

seeds floating quietly
at the tide's edge.
Distant scent of rain,

and, finally, black-
berries: dusty
and cob web-strewn,

the very sweetest far
back among the canes,
threading down through

red-leaved dogwood.
And we two, feeling
the press of time,

risk the dangerous
fabric, eager
for the pungent fruit.

2

For the pungent fruit
will soon be gone,
may already be gone

by the time we stretch
into the shadows,
though the sun still

layers its traveled light
warmly onto our backs,
urging us to embrace joy

with the short reach we have.
In the under-story,
in the space the tide

leaves, it is cool, dark
and humid. Below
the whine of insects,

and the fussing of
small brown birds,
rank mud littered

with debris, scattered bones,
last year's broken
canes. So that it seems

a miracle when our eyes
draw back again to where
the ripe berries hang.

3

Where the ripe berries hang
becomes the end of our
desire. We fill our pails

with the best we can find—
our fingers stained,
arms scratched—thinking

of morning cereal
with milk and fruit,
evening, purple gracing

rich white ice cream.
Tomorrow we'll leave:
time is relentless—kind

in its way—moments
of sweetness
brief, but growing on

these persistent roots,
that will return
years to come. And so, we

promise to return, to stand
here again,
arms reaching out,

careless of who may see
what we take before
the weather has turned.

David Filer

Sketch: Dandelions

lines so delicate
touch of any thought
will lift them away
to some nearby field

wry hand cunning eye
render the simple
weed into complex
possibility

thin white follicles
ready for release
movement sensation
heat elevating

now the dance begins
wish light fantasy
whimsical as wind
they take this new course

unruly passions
drawn out of nowhere
displacing duty
in art's fine moment

Event of Note: March 27, 2004

So sudden, it's still
hard to believe, not
yet possible to
believe. Time collapsed.
His glasses still on
the kitchen table,
slippers on the stairs,
crossword half finished,
stock tabulations
waiting for the close
that would never come.

Neighbors say it was
paramedics who
tried CPR, then
took him away. I
say they were duped. These
are mean times. I say
kidnappers, and he's
out there somewhere still,
biding his time, as
he's learned to over
his many years, not
hurt and not frightened,
or not saying so.

Someday, the service
over, when we think
it's all behind us,
the note will come, his
cursive still neat and
no more shaky than
before:

> *Son, please don't
> worry. I am as
> well as I have right
> to expect. I'm 90,*

> *after all. I don't*
> *do much with my time*
> *anyway. But I*
> *do want to mention—*
> *forgive me, I think*
> *I have once or twice*
> *before: the mail goes*
> *both ways, and if I*
> *remember, I wrote*
> *the last letter—weeks*
> *ago, I believe.*
>
> *So, if you have time*
> *(I know you're busy),*
> *let me know how you*
> *are doing, what you*
> *hear from Curran (he*
> *does remember to*
> *write, you know), how long*
> *you expect to work*
> *(your mother and I*
> *retired when we were*
> *your age), or just*
> *any news. And, as*
> *the mail goes both ways,*
> *I'll write you back (and,*
> *Promptly).*
>   *Love,*
>   *Father*

That's it. It doesn't
require ransom (or
he won't say it does).
No comment about
the new hearing aids
we talked him into.
And he's dead right, too.
His letter is there
on my desk, and no,

The Fear of Love

I haven't answered.
(But surely not weeks!)
I meant to just last
weekend. I wouldn't
have put it off past
Sunday afternoon,
but Laura's call came
on Saturday, and
then it was too late.

So, I'm writing now.
Address? Wherever.

> *I work, but fewer*
> *hours now. It's not*
> *like being retired,*
> *but the pay is good,*
> *and the schedule's mine*
> *to control. Curran*
> *keeps in touch by phone*
> *or email, as good*
> *as writing in the*
> *modern world (for those*
> *who've agreed to buy*
> *a computer). He*
> *bought a condo near*
> *Wrigley Field and has*
> *a girlfriend he seems*
> *serious about.*
> *Chicago is good*
> *for him, it appears.*
> *We plan a visit*
> *this July 4*th *for*
> *a Cubs game (you might*
> *have gone, too if you'd*
> *been willing to fly,*
> *and didn't prefer*
> *the Dodger games on*
> *your radio). So,*

not much going on.
Spring, of course, meaning
rain on and off, cold
still much of the time,
but also, tulips,
cherry trees in bloom
up and down the streets,
all the things that make
our long winters worth
living through.

  And that
reminds me, I miss
you already. (I've
never said that to
you before.) I feel
suddenly out on
the edge of something,
some void that wasn't
there before.

  If you
have really gone from
here to wherever
that is, tell me what
you see and what I
should do now that I'm
the surviving son.

I'll close now, but if
there's anything I
can do, anything
at all, I'll do it.
Now. And as you once
said, the mail goes both
ways. And I hope it
always will.
   Your son,
    David.

Aubade

The cat has been out all night,
and comes in, quickly,
looking for a place to sleep.

There has been light snow,
settled into the frozen grass
up to its brown tips. Soft

dawn light on Mt. Jefferson
to the west. An hour will pass
before the house begins to warm.

A sharp wind curls in from
the canyon, and like a stranger's
unexpected touch, reminds me

that even your anger
would be welcome company
on this late winter day.

                Redmond Oregon, 1986

David Filer

Storm Front

Storm crossed our island, the river
Somewhere upstream, the shear
Cliffs to the east. Rain shivered

The house early, before light.
But by mid-day, the sky cleared
For an hour, water glowed like

Sunset in front of fall-fired
Cottonwoods. Blue herons searched
The shallows. The kingfisher read

The falling surface from its perch.
We hunted with them, our talk
Careful, circumspect. We worked

Uneasily, as if stalked
By last night's weather. We cleared
What we could. Yet, the sun will set

Far to the south, and what was here
Last night circles and rumbles
Dark in the Oregon hills, stirs

The afternoon wind. Sparrows
And juncos crowd the feeders,
As the daylight narrows.

Travel Notes

View

a few trees bloom
on the hill beyond
the battalion fence

pink tissue blossoms

early sunlight

cluster of hot
insects among pale
pink
stones

old ruins

a warm wind
blows rain
across the strait

by afternoon
tire ruts harden
crack
there is dust

the first year in a strange land passes
into the next

the mind roots
flowers

breaks through into
what it knows

if what we are
ceases
now

David Filer

it will not be
incomplete

                Kavak Turkey, Spring 1968

The Fear of Love

While Reading James' *The Golden Bowl* at the Bus Stop

Clear and cold at dawn,
the noon sun lifted
a red-tailed hawk above
MLK Boulevard:

perfectly controlled
circles rising through
uncomplicated
air, its eyes marking

instantly the place
and range of prey lulled
into the open
by the gathering warmth.

David Filer

Calle Garcia Vigil

On the walk down, we were startled
by something flying. Neither of us
saw it, but we heard, and paused
when the shadow crossed in front,
then disappeared into other shadows.

We were walking beside a white
stucco wall broken by shuttered
windows with magenta frames.
You had been saying something
about the next street over, how
sound is like a river, another wall.

At the corner, a doorway, flanked
by dry fountains. From there, the street
descended in rows of cobblestones,
down to where lines of tall elms
covered the Zocalo like a net.
You had been talking about hope,
how it drifts through the cross-streets
and settles like dust on the sidewalks.

There was a cathedral in the next block,
its saint not well known or wealthy,
no gold or bas-relief in its nave.
You had been saying something about
promises, how they gather like
dry leaves in the courtyard, in niches
beside the thick-planked doors.

It was early October, warm,
the beginning of the dry season.
We had the address of a small
restaurant and were not far away.
You had been saying something
about love, how it drifts, at times,
like a river or dust, and how
sometimes it startles like a shadow,

or like a small dusk-gray dove,
wings whistling as it flies.
You had been saying something,
then, when the shadow stopped us,
and when we walked on, down
the cobbled street toward the Zocalo,
the sounds of the city fluttered
in the elms like captured birds.

        Oaxaca Mexico

David Filer
Bugby Hole

The river shoulders
against high Oregon
cliffs and digs itself
eighty-five feet down:
cold water rising
later like troubling
thoughts of death. Only
Bugby fishes there.

The Fear of Love

Poem Addressed to Passengers on the Downtown Bus

4 o'clock. The man
beside you reads
the Evening Tribune.
His rusty smell jostles
against your thoughts.

Your stop is next.
You will get off.

The act will be easy:
the stop cord pulled,
a light push, doors
hissing open, and then
you are free for
the short walk home.

Tomorrow
you will awaken
in a barren place.

The season
is turning.
The mocking bird
and scrub jay
know it first.
They shriek and spar
for territory
in the pepper tree.

A fresh rain.
There is yard work
to do.

You will be surprised
by your great thirst.

David Filer

The man beside you
lurches, begs
your pardon:
he can mend things,
but this time, he rises
to let you pass.

Return Trip

To Curran

The best I could do,
over Chinese dinner, was tell
you that we had to move—
it was time anyway, I said,
to find our own house,
to own property—and if she
preferred living alone,
that was her choice.

Then the long drive
to the island, only to discover
I did not have house keys.

You never complained and
slept, at least I thought
it was sleeping, all the way
back, head stiff against
the hard door, confident
that, however late, I could
take us wherever we had to go.

While I fought doubt
and tried to see what was out
there in the darkness
for both of us.

Years later, you most of
a continent away and making
decisions for your own life,
I am still humbled by your
silent trust and that you
take me—no easy companion—
with you as you go.

David Filer

Cathlamet Pastoral

It is nearly silent
in The Dock
at eight o'clock,
Saturday night, under
a wasting August
sky.

What sunset remains
west of Tenasillahe
Island is the color
of the tavern's ale.

Its window
frames a small sailboat
running back
toward the marina
on the remaining
wind.

Green and red buoy
lights just visible
where the channels
join at Steamboat Reach.

It cannot be silent,
though, as long
as that couple
at the bar disagrees
on whether it is right
to tip a Skamokawa
restaurant waitress
who has brought a bad
meal. *Gratuity*, one
says, *look it up
in the dictionary.*

Or the old guy pulling
history from his
creased face remembers
the offer to coach
the Wahkiakum Mules
he turned down in '61
to stay in Spokane.

Or as long as Naselle,
downriver,
has trouble with its school—
this Fall some kids
going on down
to Ilwaco, some
to a private school
in Astoria. *You don't
want to make
those Finns mad.*

The sound of this dark room
mutters through beer
and river talk, like flotsam,
swirling under black
pilings, down along the Brusco
tug with its tow-lights lit.

Like the heron's
awkward silhouette,
headed up to Jackson
Slough.

Like Rod Stewart
on the jukebox,
again.

Like Nancy, just
one drink shy of drunk,
but too proud

David Filer

to take a ride
home, singing back
into our night:
*I love you. I love
you all, anyway.*

                  Cathlamet Washington

The Jazz at Jimmy Mak's

To Curran, 1999

I see you, my now-grown son,
gathering your bags in Atlanta,
the South's long sounds still

warm in mid-November. You've
traveled farther, but always
with a round-trip ticket in your hand.

☾

I hope the jazz at Jimmy Mak's
is with you as you step out onto
the sidewalk looking for a cab.

☾

It's been years like this, setting
you off toward something
neither of us knew for sure.

Opening some door, urging you
along. Standing back. Now
you elbow through doors you've

opened by yourself. Twenty-two
years, untroubled by doubt. I hope
the jazz at Jimmy Mak's is with you.

☾

Listen. It's 9:30. Mel Brown's
quintet is half-way through the first
set, trumpet and tenor trading short

David Filer

breaks on "Windjammer,"
Louis Pain's Hammond growling
subtly in support. It's Thursday,

a steady rain rolling down Everett
Street. Cold. Winter has returned
to the Northwest, and already it seems

like it's been here forever. The club
is filling up, though, the bar
crowded, only the tables near the stage

aren't reserved. The room is warm
and well-dressed, and there's an
under-tone that seems like part of the act.

◯

Listen. 10:30 and Thara's at it again,
drum and bass behind him, up close
to the mike, scatting through his horn,

the raspy words telling some intricate
story, a long, earthy poem
only he and the women understand.

◯

If you were here, I'd ask about your
new job, and you'd have plenty to say.
The father, I'd set our theme, see

where you could take it from there,
my comments, spare and wise,
noodling in the spaces that you'd leave.

The Fear of Love

○

Listen. Now it's Mel himself taking
off on "Pygmy," setting down that funky,
funky beat, improvising, snare and top hat,

on his old Motown rhythms, the band
relaxing, taking a drink, waiting
for the moment it's given back. Listen.

○

Wherever you go in the years to come,
remember the jazz at Jimmy Mak's. The next
set will just be starting when you return.

David Filer

Travel Notes

El Golfo de Santa Clara

The wind squalls, dawn
to dusk, then back again
at night. Sand furrows
grow along the tidal flat.
Spring weather. I appear,
smiling like a new moon
in the brief evening calm.
My dreams, winnowed by day,
retreat into a fair selvage
guaranteed to the next
wind change.

Sunset

In time, everything
will reach this: sun's edge to earth,
daytime and then night.

Sea Level

Midnight.
The tide changes
imperceptibly. Shrimp
boats ease keel and gunwale
into the mud. Remnants of the Colorado spread,
searching like roots for
sea level. The wind
off the gulf splays
sand against our tent
where we sleep confirmed
in half-visions of tidal
concentrations.

Packing

Gathering the tent
and living gear,
we leave the beach
with vague imprints
of our machinations.

Tecate Summit

The climb to Tecate
summit, even in this
season, demands attention.
Radiator water set out
at each half mile. Creosote
and sage fill out to
chaparral. As we rise,
the gulf, left far behind,
is released by the moon
and returns, like time,
thinning, a worn mirror
through which we discover
that our strangeness is
a space opening ahead,
and getting home is only
where the trip begins.

David Filer
Postcard from Shaniko

We discover it as
if it were new.
The hotel is strewn
with old men. They come
down from well-
cleaned rooms,
cross the lobby
and disappear.

They know their duty.
Wait. Wear down.
In time they will
be invisible.

        One mutters
that he would insist...
but the rest is garbled
and in some other tongue.

Another picks up
pieces of white bone.
He is saving them
but has forgotten
where.

        A radio plays
loud western music.

There will be rain in Portland,
chance of thunderstorms
east of the Cascades tonight.

The Fear of Love

Someone writes,
    "Dear Ones,
    We are well. Your
    father has his mind
    made up, though.
    He will become
    obscure. Take care
    of yourselves."

The grizzled head
understands that we
are not dreaming.
His fugitive smile
rises like dust.

Someone sings,
    "You'll come back.
    You will come back."

Clearly
this time.

    Shaniko Oregon, 1974

David Filer

Japanese Garden, Portland Oregon

To Curran and Young

spring maples
light beyond
light coming through
light under
branched veins
indeterminate pulse
the moment
all this

Photographs

Colette, Le Verdon s/Mer

Summer has gone,
quietly,
from salt marsh, scrub pines
grass-fringed dunes,

gone from the empty beach
silver with sand and fine
shell fragments,
gone from tidal rocks,
the green-gray mist
where the Gironde
meets the sea.

In this picture,
her face can be seen,
dark eyes serious,
patient with the past
but carefully seeing beyond,
as if she can make out
where light and dark
come together.

Self-portrait, Redmond

Here the season has changed too, cottonwoods in the canyon edged with yellow, juncos in and out of the feeder, ticking songs echoing as if on wires, dry elm leaves on the ground.

The face is lost in the window, each feature brushed with shadow and reflection. It is easier to see out than in, and as sunlight fades against the peaks in the West, the scene dissolves to another life.

1986

David Filer
Self-Guided

Finally, tired of the tour,
The plausible explanations,

Background voices, camera flashes,
We lagged back, stared for a while

At the last diorama,
The still-life figures staring

Back. Then left and sat outside
By the museum pond, a pair

Of mallards feeding, up-ended,
In the bottom muck. We sat

Outside in the cooling air, and said
Not much at all. While above,

A late September sky grew
Dismal, under fast, icy clouds.

                Victoria British Columbia

It Happened

It happened
Saturday when they
were stopped on their way
by the black and white-
striped crossing arms—
Portland, 12th Avenue,
Clinton Street, Masonry
Supply on the right,
county building on
the left—bells and flashing
red lights between them
and where they wanted
to go.

    He
set the brake, shut off
the motor, removed
his glasses and sat
back. The diesel horn's
rising pitch took his
thoughts upward with each
advancing wave, until
as the engines passed,
he rose so high above
it all that he drifted
north-northeast with the
prevailing wind.

    She
noticed he had gone
but stared ahead, watched
the line of freight rumble
by, blurred blacks, blues,
browns, chaotic cartoons,
strange graffiti words,
found herself voicing
an old childhood game—

David Filer

boxcar, flatcar, tankcar,
boxcar, flatcar

—then, without waiting
for the caboose, pulled
down the visor mirror,
checked her makeup, looked
back down the growing
line of cars, got out
and walked away.

        Later, they
recalled how it had been,
when, growing impatient,
he turned her way to
see if the end was in
sight,

saw her
smile, and then the small
tear crossing on her cheek.

Weather Notes

How like the rain
        to fall when the earth
lacks moisture how
like it to fall
        in season and out.

○

I thought it might be the sun
        but it was only a white
curtain dancing
in the morning breeze.

○

If you were the wind
you would be from the west now
backing to southwest then south
the scent of dry
leaves in your hair
willow and ash.

○

This time of year
fog early
        means clear
afternoons sharp
angled light keeping
        the buildings
from collapse.

○

When I saw that thin
stream of smoke against
the first snow
on Mt. Hood

David Filer

I remembered how
it was to dance
as if we
were not breathing.

◯

A rainbow surrounds
         you angles precise
between the sun your body
and my eye.

◯

How like the rain to be down
         in the gutter at midnight singing
like an old drunk
who's forgotten
how to get home.

◯

How like the rain
to have the last word
rattling on the roof
as we slip off
to sleep.

Itinerary

Seat belt signs are off,
cruising altitude
32,000 feet.

United Flight 628,
heading nearly due east,
Portland to Chicago-

O'Hare. Above, a light
haze that obscures most of
Washington, Idaho,

rumbles up into a
towering summer storm-
front over Utah,

then thins out again
and breaks here and there
to reveal patterns

familiar from our previous
crossings, South Dakota's
dark scrub hills and gritty

canyons, creeks already
dry in July, giving
way to something more kempt

in Iowa, plowed squares
and rectangles pocked
by cloud shadows, straight

county roads, houses
and barns in their marked
corners, a few small towns.

David Filer

◯

The Missouri, and now
we start to think about
why we headed this way,

begin to remember
where we put our baggage,
consider our small spaces.

Time collapses against
us like a quantum wave,
and we are in all

places at once as we
move into past and future.
As the soul, sometimes,

in its free-ranging flight
sees in the space below
how life is configured—

how it is in the moment
it spreads and swirls back,
how it begins in dark,

unravels into light
and how it threads back
into the coming twilight.

◯

It is as you once said,
nothing lasts but something
like light moves ever toward

us, even as the same
light moves away. Thus our
continual dilemma,

on sleeping and then
waking, looking ahead
and sorry for the time

we so spend, mourning
what we have lost in the
spaciousness of our dreams

while aching for deliverance.
So we ask for time to
continue on and wish

for it to start over
again, that we may finally
get the memories

right, get the meaning right,
order the details
before we forget them all,

◯

as we propel ourselves
forward into the next
day, while behind us

the day we have just
lived separates again
into its various moments,

one of which—all of which
we follow, looking both ways
into raveling time.

We ask only another
day, and already we
fly against it on our

David Filer

way to what we could
not imagine even
days ago. First the light

then, increasingly,
the dark, the wings out
there flashing warnings

now, as below us,
across the horizon
and on beyond our

sight, town after town
begins to shine like
a prairie of stars.

Atcheson, Topeka and Santa Fe

It must have been the 30's—
dire winds of poverty
whirling people about like
elm leaves—that left them out there
in the high desert, their home
a work train on the southwest
line.

      Gallup, New Mexico,
no glib swing song there, no pearls,
no silk stockings on that siding
of their lives: snapping day heat
and freezing nights, tending store
for spikers, gandydancers,
gypsies of the long iron rails,
everyone too far from home.

I see my mother, bucket
of coal in her twenty-two
year old hands, fresh from college,
her precious knowledge useless
because it did not instruct
on firing a cast-iron stove.

I know, now, she would have been
beautiful, squatting there, cold
and confused, the desert vast
behind her in the night—know
her beauty would not have been
stories and the thousand real
comforts of motherhood, still
years—Blythe and Indio—ahead:

but haunches, spreading like Spring
from her slim waist, delicate breasts
poised over the dusty coal,
a bitter scent hovering
in the sliding steel doorway,

David Filer

her sex molten with anger
ready to be taken off
to a sweeter landscape, scent
of oranges and sweet daphne
gentle in some evening air.

Three Wedding Quatrains

Who thought such surly skies and heavy air
Could yield, through devotion, a garden here?
Strange summer, in a world withered with gloom,
We witness Young and Curran join and bloom.

How nervous, as if it were my huge step
He's taking. Resigned to watch, yes, I wept.
Bride's mother, too, feelings in disarray:
Pride, joy and worry, on this wedding day.

Flying home, it's cloudy across two time zones.
I sit in silence, as if I'm alone.
How amazing: born, then grown in a wink.
I'd better watch this Bond film and not think.

      Chicago, August 19, 2006

David Filer

The Mortals of Keşan

in the stare of the eye
behind the iris
behind the clear pool
is the pool
still,
muted,
sufficient, floating the leaves
of dry oaks

string kites
in the wind
light times in the brevity
in the dusty streets
salty peanuts—5 lira

the mind sees nothing
but reflections
in the pool
where the wind is vacant
and the dry leaves
float forever

the wind in the streets
passes through the world I love you
I long to write what is
between
what is the wind
and the word
and fly the word
high in the wind
over the streets

from the pool
behind the pool
not looking at but remembering
what the wind shakes
from the oak

change: let it happen the world
looks back into
the eye opening
the eyes sees nothing but the pool
behind the eye

not itself, but something
must happen must
keep the kite high
the string taut

it is in the possibility
of the memory that the
eye selects the word
and offers it for change
sacrifice

variously, as the leaf
shimmering between
the word and the wind

this is how I love you
this is how I tell you so
this is why she comes
to the well, wrinkled,
covered in black but for
her eyes,
this is why she fills the bucket
to fill in turn the pool

turning the oaken crank,
the rope-wind widens
turn by turn and the bucket
comes to the surface

then the word comes away
from the well as the wind
turns the crank

David Filer

and the bucket pauses
in her hand familiar
with the form of each other
worn by each other

the mortals of Keşan—
dusty in the streets,
following wind-kites
growing older
shopping, looking,
in the window of the eye
into the windows
of the pool

floating older
from the oak settling
into the pool

this is the way I love you
this is the way I tell you so

              Turkey, 1967

Aubade

To Marlene
             July 5, 2006

We wake early, dawn still gray
outside the curtains, alarm
even before our neighbor's
noisy dogs. We've done this wrong

to ourselves—plane to catch, you'll
be half-way around the world
before you stop. So these fleet
moments seem worth savoring,

saving, not as if they might
be our last (no, don't think it),
rather just the few that we can
share now.

             But now you are gone,

and I'm watching the daylight's
gradual ebb, swallows nipping
midges from the cool air—all that
half-a-world from you, but in

the moment you woke and left.
I hope you've saved it too, packed
it to Sabaki village,
and so we'll wake together,

however distant we may
be, dawn not compelling
us to anything but love—
while our homeward journeys wait.

David Filer

Portland Time

I see you now, as your plane lifts and climbs,
Our seconds splitting into here and there.
You said you'd keep your watch on Portland time.

It's always like this when you leave: separate time
And space growing between us—here and there.
I see you there, now: heat waves lift and shine.

You shade your eyes, watching an eagle climb,
Serengeti's hot winds blowing your hair.
You said you'd keep your watch on Portland time.

And it's precisely now in both our times,
Yours half a world away—your here, my there.
I see you there, as our futures shift and climb.
I hope you've kept your watch on Portland time.

Shining Back

I see you there, shading your eyes, the evening Serengeti sun
    shimmering
In the day's remaining heat. Something is out there, soaring,
    or gathering around
A carcass, or knee-deep in a watering hole. It doesn't matter.
    It's all too
Far off and lost in diminishing layers, the plain blending into
    the sunset
Beyond the farthest point that you can see. There, in that farther
    landscape, is what you came for:
The other, the out-of-place, the grain that is the least and most
    of what can be seen.
And it is there, shining back with its own light into your eyes.
    I see you turning,
Climbing into the truck, the dusty road, the clear, cold earth-
    circling air, touching down
In our green Northwest, what you've seen still there, as you come
    toward me and your eyes meet mine.

David Filer

Diminishing

    i

In the air now, straight lines of gray snow,
Rain pushing down through just-freezing air.
Snow, the way I like it, on the verge
Of warming back into rain. I try
To remember what you said you'd be
Doing that day, what it sounded like,
Turning to wonder, and maybe that
Was the place I stopped and looked across
The water, looked through the snow, or what
Was left of it, and saw lights coming
Down the river, just lights, red, green, white,
Ghostly at this distance, and yet real,
As if memory might be enough,
With more winter weather coming on.

    ii

Back then, I probably called it hopeful,
The way, suddenly, there were pale green
Leaves on our maples, and a soft haze
Penetrated the cooling sunshine.
It was on such a late Spring evening—
No, it was that very Spring evening,
I turned left off Bybee and slowed at
The crosswalk, just past the old Moreland,
And after how many years, I thought of you,
How the vibrant light of the neon
Around the theater's deco marquee
Was like your blue eyes. But then farther down
Milwaukie, waiting behind the 19 Bus,
I could not be sure either had been true.

Since You Asked

Yes, the mergansers are still here,
but they won't be long.
Winter is calling, and they hear
it as an old song.

I should leave too. It's winter
singing its cold song.
Yes, the mergansers are still here,
but they won't be for long.

Postscripts

Late Elegy

A great blue, hunched at the edge of an ebbing
Tide, background of ravens working the mud flat,
Gull on the left, wings folded, waiting—all screened
By rain, as a quiet day comes to its end.

Like last March did, but gentler, with only
Gentle loss. Is it an answer, this drawing
In of deckled clouds, spring storm in the alders
Just turning green, Canada geese, a dozen or
More, crossing far off into the fading sky?

We can't be sure we love things when they are near
And cannot be forgotten. But now, there's your
Grizzled face, when we try to remember it,
Your voice on those unexpected calls, urging
Us to visit, or was it saying good-bye?

To Neal
    March 2005

David Filer

Taken

I take my time reading Richard Wilbur,
Captured by his wit, playful yet sober.

A verbal nudge, a sly pun, almost fey,
As if he knew I couldn't turn away,

Would be entranced by joy as well as grief,
His measured trust in love, however brief.

More now as my hair has turned to silver,
I take my time and read Richard Wilbur.

Epitaph in Advance

If there were time enough not to care,
I'd write more lines than just this pair.

Poem Notes

Most of the poems in the Snow Down River section are set in (but not necessarily about) the landscape of Puget Island in the lower Columbia River.

In "Mood Indigo" and "Cathlamet Pastoral," The Dock is (or was) a tavern in Cathlamet Washington on the lower Columbia River (bridge connection to Puget Island).

The settings for "Still Life," "View," and "The Mortals of Keşan" are small towns in western Turkey, which the author had the pleasure of being stationed near while serving in the U.S. Army in the late 1960's.

"Funambulist" was inspired by an article in The New Yorker about the famous French tight-rope walker (funambulist) Phillippe Petit.

"Triangulation" accounts for the location of the author's son Curran and father Neal in the Fall of 1995 after Curran had started college at Bucknell University. "Triangulation" is a navigational process whereby bearings on known locations yield the location of an unknown location (the navigator's.)

"Sonnets to My Father" was written while the author's father lived in Ojai, California and had survived heart surgery at age 84. The last line of the second sonnet has changed a few times to account for his age, but will not change further.

The poem "August: A Vow" became a poem in honor of the author's son Curran's marriage to Young Jee Son on the date indicated. The author's hope was that it recognized the sweetness of the relationship and the desire that it would endure, risks notwithstanding. See also, "Three Wedding Quatrains."

"Bugby Hole" is located (and so-named on the NOAA navigational chart) on the lower Columbia River, where the river is deflected to the northwest by a basalt cliff.

The setting for "The Jazz at Jimmy Mak's" is a well-known live-jazz nightclub in Portland Oregon. The musicians mentioned—Mel Brown, Thara Memory and Louis Pain—were part of the regular Thursday night band, The Mel Brown Quintet.

The setting for "Postcard from Shaniko" is a very small town in central Oregon. In 1974, when the author visited on a photography trip, the Shaniko Hotel was used for an assisted living facility for mentally impaired elderly.

The occasion for "Japanese Garden" was a visit by the author, the author's wife, the author's son and his wife to the Japanese Garden in Portland's Washington Park.

The nominal location for "It Happened" is where SE 12th Avenue in Portland Oregon is crossed by the Santa Fe Burlington Northern main line, resulting in frequent traffic delays.

The setting for "Atcheson, Topeka & Santa Fe" is the author's imagined version of the setting for his father's and mother's first post-college employment in the 1930's, running a general store on a work train run by the named railroad.

The poems "Aubade," "Portland Time" and "Shining Back" in the Travel Notes section, all relate to the author's wife's project in Kenya, described in the Author Note. The short villanelle form used in "Portland Time" was modeled on Donald Justice's poem, "Women in Love."

"Late Elegy," in the Postscripts section, was written a year after the death of the author's father.

About the Author

Photo by Marlene Anderson

David Filer was raised in the low California desert and has lived in Oregon since 1975. Now retired from teaching and the law, he splits his time between his home in Portland and his second home on Puget Island in the lower Columbia River. His wife Marlene Anderson created and perpetuates The Imani Project, an AIDS prevention education, medical and orphan support project in villages on the Indian Ocean coast of Kenya (www.imaniproject.org). Previous publications include chapbooks titled *Night Verse*, from Finishing Line Press (2005), *The Landscape There*, from Stone City Press (2009), *Weather Patterns*, from Dancing Moon Press (2011), and *Housekeeping*, from Finishing Line Press (2012).

www.ingramcontent.com/pod-product-compliance
Lightning Source LLC
Chambersburg PA
CBHW052101070526
44584CB00017B/2289